Tips for Domestic Travel

Black Lawrence Press
www.blacklawrence.com

Executive Editor: Diane Goettel
Book Design: Steven Seighman

Black Lawrence Press
8405 Bay Parkway C8
Brooklyn, N.Y. 11214
U.S.A.

Some of these poems appeared in slightly different forms in the following publications:

5 A.M.: "Day Players in the Makeup Trailer," "RX 2005"
Rattle: "Self-Portrait With the Smithfield Ham We Had to Cut on the Bandsaw"
Drunken Boat: "Fact or Fiction," "Your Suicide Script"
Margie: "Hospice Symptom Relief Kit," "21st Century Options," "Waking,"
Nimrod: "Tips For Domestic Travel"
Philadelphia Stories: "Renovation," "Colloquy in the Heat," "Midway"
Mad Poets Review: "The Ship of Grief Returns to Shore," "I'm Sorry to Tell You."

"Clothesline" first appeared in the anthology *Hands Offering Bread* (Bucks County Poet Laureate Program). "The Book of Years," "Self-Portrait With the Smithfield Ham..." and "Tips for Domestic Travel" won the Robert Fraser Poetry Award in 2005.

Cover painting: "Untitled," by Stirling Spadea

Published 2009 by Black Lawrence Press, an imprint of Dzanc Books

First edition 2009

Printed in the United States

TIPS
for
DOMESTIC
TRAVEL

poems by
Hayden Saunier

Black Lawrence Press
New York

CONTENTS

I

II

III

IV

for
my mother and father
and
Abby, Sam, and Reb

I

TIPS FOR DOMESTIC TRAVEL

If you walk up, weeping, to an airline counter
one hour before flight and three days after

elevated warnings of terrorist attacks,
you should expect the body search

of a lifetime, even if you aren't wearing
an underwire bra. If you are, expect the sounds

that emanate from your breasts to summon
additional personnel and bomb-sniffing dogs

to the scene. Gloved women will work a wand
around your chest, ponder beeps and whines,

while men unpack your underwear, unzip
your tampon pouch. Impossible to think

someone could be dying during this. Bereft
of wristwatch, car keys, spare change, you walk

through portals, your shoes beside you, traveling
a scuffed black river in a plastic tub—

isn't this the way we keep death at bay?
By taking off our clothes? Of course, someone

is dying; someone is dying as you wait,
as you walk; someone is dying as you enter

the glassed-off security box, assume the requested
wide-legged stance. You lift your arms out wide,

as though for the embrace you're traveling
toward, the one that won't arrive,

but you don't know that, all you know is
you're the image sent in capsules

into outer space: Leonardo's Vitruvian Man,
alarms singing on both sides of your heart.

RENOVATION

I ripped the carpet off my stairs
so now I'm halfway up and halfway
down, extracting staples from scarred
slabs of pumpkin pine, thinking
how destruction beats creation
in a footrace every day—heave
most things out an upstairs window,
gravity will do the rest—but this work
has me on my knees and keeps me there
and what I bow before keeps changing:
hail to staple guns and staples,
hail the work of opposition, *hail*
determination of the soul
who put this carpet down that it
should be eternal, *hail* my kneepads,
needle-nosed pliers, teeth, *hail*
my flathead screwdriver shaft
that pries and lifts these staples up
like bodies out of earth, *hail*
to the ding they sing to the pail,
to sanding and to grit, to elbow grease,
to oil, to spreading polyurethane
across the treads like honey with a brush,
to watching as it sinks into the grain
four times before it lies atop the surface,
do not touch, until it's formed
the recommended hard, bright shine.

DAY PLAYERS IN THE MAKEUP TRAILER

I'm sitting in between a dead girl and a prostitute.
I play a nurse—no nonsense—powder, touch of lips,
"those test results you wanted just came in"
then they'll be done with me. I shake hands
with the prostitute. The dead girl pulls a curtain
back, says "what the hell, there's nudity, so what?"
She's eighteen, grey-blue, naked and they're gluing
latex lacerations on her neck and shoulders,
building up contusions, painting gorgeous bruises
down her arms. She's never done a film before.
She tells us that she's hoping for a line,
that maybe when they see her they'll decide
to let her speak, create a flashback or a dream scene,
shoot a memory of who she was, alive.
The prostitute and I say nothing.
We tilt our chins up for the final brush.
The dead girl's voice trails off. They blue her lips.
I look reliable, the prostitute looks hard-mouthed,
sad-eyed sexy and the dead girl's looking dead.
We're done now, all of us. We're going on.

CLEANING OUT THE ATTIC, I SING LONG OVERDUE PRAISE TO BIG SHIRTS

O Big Shirts,
let me proclaim your greatness
as I unpack you from this broken-zippered suitcase
I should have thrown away
but couldn't, owing as I did, my life
to you, a full year of my life,

Heroic Shirts!
You were protectors,
muumuus, blankets, friends,
clothes that swaddled
and unswaddled both,
shirts of my father,
shirts of my brothers,
shirts of the Big and Tall,

O, when I lifted you,
you tents, cloaks, awnings, sacks,
you burkas of the West,
above my head, and slid you
down onto my frame,
no one had a clue
of what was underneath you,
your great sleeves
so accommodating to bandages
and sling, to the healing
of defensive wounds

and later, with your front breast pocket
pendulous with wallet, keys, an orange,
anything, so long as it hung down,
swung low like an Amazonian tit

or hint of colostomy bag,
together we kept half the world away,
Magnanimous Shirts!

Wrapped in your voluminous magic,
I traveled through my days invisibly,
a head and ankles— I thought and moved,
unlooked at and un-lusted after—
a truck with mud flaps,
gigantic shirttails lapping at my heels.

O Shirts,
I bathe you, dry you, starch and iron you,
stroke your collars, smooth your plackets,
button up your cuffs in praise.
I sing your stripes and solids, puce
and umbers, lurid plaids and tropic prints,
Egyptian cotton, polyester blends
and drive you through these city streets
toward the thrift shop,
Mighty shirts!

May you be strong and righteous;
May your future be bright and clean;
May you be fitting decorations for the placid backs
of robust men and women;
May you take your place as shirts, not shields—
except against ordinary sun,
against the daily glancing knife blades of the cold.

TABLE

Here we heard the story of how we almost never were.
We were eating chicken, rice and butter beans.

Father was flying, both wings dead with ice
above the tidal marshes, no solid ground

inside the magic circle of his calculations,
for him, the center point, to land,

so we were falling too. We felt ourselves

begin to disappear, the plates to tremble, milk
to slosh inside our cups, we banked

hard left and watched the biscuit basket
sliding past the fruit bowl, watched our sticky

rice-flecked hands steam prints that vanished
from the tabletop, we stalled and spiraled

down into the center of his cautionary tale—

below us, turbulence; legs twisting, kicking,
brothers crying, my sister trying not to pee—

until at last he dove toward the smokestacks
of a rendering plant, where we are lifted

by the heat of horses' hooves and hides, ice
melting off, wings clear, we wing it home,

our lives intact, our lesson learned,

our landing smooth as the imperturbable surface
of a Mother's chocolate silk pie.

FLIP DOLL: RED RIDING HOOD

You won't find legs beneath
this dolly's blue flecked gingham skirt.
Or feet. No, there's a cast of characters
below, connected at the waist
and rather intimately, wouldn't you agree?
Good God! What kind of toy
is this to give a girl? Don't try to tell me
this is anatomically correct.

I flip Red on her head—
her skirt turns green and fifty years
fly by—it's grandma! with impressive
sagging breasts, grey curls like painted waves
across her brow. She wears a nightcap.
Pull it down to cover up her wrinkled face,
then turn her over—ho, ho, ho, it's wolf.

He wears the nightcap now,
dress buttoned high to hide the apple
in his throat, that tell-tale scrap of red cape
in his mouth's a tongue. Red's upside down,
below, her pig tails touching earth.
And here's the kicker, if you want to play—
no woodsman. Save yourself.

COLLOQUY IN THE HEAT

Next door, Osiris howls
in short odd yips; he never barks.
Being trapped inside the body
of a Siberian Husky in the August heat
is better, perhaps, than being shoved
alive into a coffin and thrown into the sea
but not by much. How it compares to
being chopped up into fourteen pieces,
some say sixteen, thrown into the Nile,
one's penis snapped up by a crocodile,
I can't say. But help me out here, Os.
Was this before or after Isis used your corpse
to get herself knocked up with Horus
and gave birth to half a dozen gods?
Either way, no wonder you made
mummification a rite of the dead.
God, Osiris, it's all too much for me:
the heat, the dead, the names
we answer to. You're tied to a post,
tongue out, regarding me
with one brown eye, one blue.
I look back from this body with this name.
Tell me: whose sound is more ill-fated?
Your short yips? Or my attempts at speech?

THE MACHINIST'S VIEW

Not knowing the sea town where you are taking
your tumor for salt air, I cobble together
a landscape from AAA maps
and English novels brought to the screen
by the BBC. Huddled cottages. Lilacs
in late spring. I lay out a curve of beach
for you to walk but now I'm stealing from
The French Lieutenant's Woman,
Meryl pale and tragic on the sea wall,
lashed by wind and all those petticoats,
patiently waiting for a plot device.
I'll give you better weather, better food, no corset,
plus both roles: the obsessed and the obsession.
Unfortunately, Jeremy Irons isn't available.
I checked. But here's some fun news: yesterday,
my neighbor told me global weather change
is caused by rocket launches! He says
several million tons of thrust can knock
a planet oh-so-slightly off its course
and then there's hell to pay.
I have to say I found it comforting,
the idea we might nudge things back
in place. Tap. Tap. Be careful on the stone path
to the beach—it's slippery and scenic—always
a tricky combination. Walk out there,
watch the water change direction.
Feel the difference one millimeter makes.

SELF-PORTRAIT WITH THE SMITHFIELD HAM WE HAD TO CUT ON THE BAND SAW

Mother, for once, it wasn't your fault.
You always said you can't soak hams
long enough and one full day and night
seemed adequate, but we gave it two,
scrubbed mold, rind, salt away, changed
the water, tucked it like a baby in its bath;
another day, rinsed, patted dry, made ready.
Butter and brown sugar coated all our hands.
Let's face it; it was ancient, not just aged.
The woman at the ham shack must have seen
my husband's Pennsylvania plates and figured
what the hell, he won't be coming back.
Or it was just bad luck. But wasn't
our discussion about life with Lewis and Clark
educational for the children? Ham jerky!
Ham shoelaces! Ham-flavored chewing gum
to last a winter portage through the Bitterroots!
Yes, we were jolly then, those spots still undiscovered
on your lungs. It's true, my Yankee husband
cut it on the band saw but so would any man
faced with that ham who had a power tool in reach.
Easter, then. November, now. You're dead.
I'm making black bean soup, beginning
with a frozen cut of that disaster
sizzling in a taste of olive oil. No other
seasoning is needed for this winter's portage,
just my store of crosscut sections:
meat and marrow, sugar, grease and bone.

NOTES TOWARD AN ODE TO BAD DECISIONS

1.

Point of departure: age six,
top of stairs.
I climb into a cardboard box
one sticky hand holding fast
to a polished spindle.
Release, push off, launch—
into complete comprehension
of gravity, inclined plane,
and the concept of irrevocable action.

2.

You.

3.

Could be a book length sequence!

4.

Include:
Running with vomiting child
and resulting lubricated slide across floor.
Storing exacto knife in pants pocket.
Moving to New York City.
Leaving New York City.
Eating oysters above bar in Galway, Ireland.
Having just one cigarette.

5.

Am I avoiding you? Details!

6.

What is normally a slow ass-busting descent
of a staircase in a sleeping bag
turned suddenly into a combo platter
of exhilaration/terror/death wish
that is the hallmark of requited lust.
Recipe: equal parts irrevocability and speed.

7.

Boone's Farm Apple Wine.
Allowing Mormon missionaries in the door.
Growing pot in a field before learning it belongs
to the Chief of Police.
Anything advertising an open mike.

8.

All right, quick review:
child, box, stairs,
man, woman, New York City,
projectile vomiting, box-cutter, oysters,
wine, missionaries, pot, open mikes.
You know
which you.

9.

Eureka!
Child careening down stairs

in cardboard box a metaphor for relationship!
Initial lack of understanding of physics
a major contributing factor!
Implications for both love
and transportation!

10.

Mathematical equation:
pain experienced
at relationship's end
must be equal to pleasure
at onset.
A staircase.

11.

Fourth floor walk up.
Macrobiotic diet.
That dinner party when the tablecloth caught fire.
Band-aiding the nipples.

12.

No landing. Open door
into the garden—
sometimes there's God—so quickly!
cries Blanche Dubois
and so it ends where it began
with your body in a box
in the deep green center of a privet hedge,
pulse pounding, some part
of your heart pierced
like a box cutter stuck deep in a thigh.
You're on your own: alive.

II

WAKING

Clockwork. Each morning
your death
waits patiently near the bed—

      not black-winged,
      hunched or hovering,

just there, in a chair
by the window
perusing *The New York Times*.

Your death's been up all night,
turning pages quietly,

      noting upcoming events,
      licking the lead
      on its pencil.

It's ready for you now.
With a handful of suggestions for your day.

BEACH

I've never found the body of a man
although the ocean takes one from the village

every year. Sometimes a rogue wave lifts
a tourist off the rocks below the lighthouse

but it's rare—most bodies never reappear.
The year the dead seal came into the cove

I thought, at first, it was a man. Such size
and bloat. No tide would take it back.

I rowed out to the carcass, pushed it into deeper
currents, but still, each morning, floating, *there*.

To hell with it, I thought, I'm used to living
with the dead; they're everywhere. I challenged: stay.

By daybreak, it was gone—ghost ship—away.
Leaving me the usual: flat sea, memory.

YOUR SUICIDE SCRIPT

came off beautifully, obeyed classic
Chekhovian rules of dramaturgy,

rule one being: if you bring a gun
onto the stage, you have to use it.

Of course, I only saw the second act,
the service in your memory

where two dozen candles burned inside
a dozen pairs of your exquisite, empty shoes.

Each flame reflected, multiplied
in the polish of your hand-sewn, two-toned,

butter-soft balmorals and wing-tipped
brogues, oxfords, loafers, dirty bucks

that promised any minute to ignite
a pyre of hide and eyelet, tassel, heel bed,

wax and wick. But didn't.
Talk wound down. Candles sputtered,

guttered in their liquid
and your shoes did what shoes do

without owners: nothing. Become
props. Leading me back to the first,

more problematic act.
Too minimalist, too bare.

That single chair. The shotgun.
And the cast of one.

BOOK OF YEARS

I took a walk across the fields last year,
a bad year, people dying on me left and right
and some years don't you find it hard to bear?
You know the ones. Their illustrations
in your childhood Book of Years
are printed from a rough-cut woodblock: figures
clad in long patched coats, bent over by the weight
of rags and sticks strapped to their backs,
plodding up a barren landscape; line, stump,
stone. The weight the figure labors under
is the point: weight, empty space and what
the chisel cut away. That kind of year. Dry-etched.
Ice-edged. The walking raw. Until I spooked
a buck who'd bedded down in chest-high grass
and he, in turn, spooked me. Hoof-thrash in
dry leaf-rattle sent me backward fast
as he came staggering through grasses, antlers
filled with rustling stalks, this yokel wakened
from his haystack nap, locked in a gaze
with an ass-down fool in an icy ditch
and somewhere, laughter? Laughter from that
chubby pink-cheeked girl who's dangling
her dimpled legs across the gold gilt frame
bordering the next illustration (castle,
river, gentle hill), smiling at you, stacks
of gooseberry tarts in hand, as if to say
all that's needed is the sense to turn the page.

UNTANGLING MARIONETTES

These poses are impossible—everyone's twisted,
back bent, trussed for butchering—a bomb's
exploded! No, just carelessness in the toy box,
a grinning clown at the center. Limbs and eyehooks
clatter as I twist the pink-tongued spaniel
until she's free of the dragon's tail. But not
the blank-eyed boy. His knees are tight against
the maiden's door knob nose, her dowel feet caught
in the clown's fake scepter, now tangled with
witch's broom. Only the dragon has the sense
to show some outrage, everyone else's mouth is
painted shut. Enough.
I snip strings, separate the bodies, lay them flat.
Dragon, dog, boy, girl, clown and crone
reconnected to their crosses, knotted,
tightened, trimmed. No unexpected moves.
Just the world, dangling from my rafter,
in the universal poses of the hanged.

WHY I PRACTICE YOGA

Each breath is a choice
between miracle
and grievance,
the yoga teacher says.

Oh make me puke, I think.

I'm flat on my back,
in *savasana*, the corpse pose,
alongside thirty other people.

We're trying to leave our bodies
while we're still alive.

I can hear you laughing now

from wherever you went
when you died.

That's good.
I've missed your laugh.

A KIND OF GEOMETRY

The old man surveys his garden,
feels earth give beneath his boots one day,
hard freeze the next.
He stares through thin electric wire wound around
old posts to keep out deer.
This is the year
he plans alone and works alone and eats alone.

His rhubarb and asparagus return, spear loam,
punch crust. Some beds
don't change. He stares.
I figure he's given up the garden.

Then, he upends posts, restrings wire,
makes a small square inside the larger one,
begins to till.
Something's worked out in his head.

The length of your ability
times the width of your need,
that's how they say you calculate a garden.
The trick is leaving depth of loss unspaded,
but no one tells you how.

THE MYSTERY OF HOUSES

How easily we walk into the house of childhood,
put our suitcase down.

The house has a face, the door is a mouth.
We enter, are consumed by scent,

each room holds its bouquet expectantly for us.
Wood smoke, mint, the tang of urine, dead ash, bread—

and everything's exactly as we left it: upturned
cup on the drain board, sugar spoon, paring

knife. Curtains lift, reveal familiar stands of trees
and when the front door slams, turn quickly,

catch the best of these theatrical effects—
ourselves, running past ourselves,

into the house, a blur, cry, gone.
No matter. We've slid our hands up

the banister, we've climbed the stairs,
we're busy peeling strips of paper back,

exposing plaster, wallboard, brick,
searching for a border of ducks and sheep,

for the complicated pattern of our parents' room.
Two hands will shutter a face. Faces fade,

old photos slipped from oval frames, crushed
velvet left beneath. But not the rooms. We remember

rooms. The way light enters now is how
it entered then. And how it fell, it falls, again.

CLOTHESLINE

She's taken the trousers down
and propped them up to soften by the fire.
They were his. She wears them.
Nothing's wasted here.

What remains outside:
a nightgown, underwear,
two sheets, a single towel
worn thin enough to dry
in this cold.

At dusk, she unpins each piece,
steps carefully across the frozen yard,
basket held on one hip as she climbs
the stairs. She makes her bed,
puts on the nightgown.

If there is snow by morning,
she'll slip her hands into his gloves,
her fingers following the curve
his fingers made. She'll hold the line
between house and barn for balance,
as she steps into the silence deep snow brings
to hammer the ice
grown thick inside the troughs.

CROSSING

The boys in their almost men's bodies are afraid
to cross the long field between cabins in the dark.

Night presses on the windows, presses on their chests.

A high moon thickens hemlock shadow,
makes the ocean lapping low cliffs glitter so the field

becomes a path between two terrors.

Eyeshine of owl and osprey on one side, relentless
ocean on the other, turning like the black

magnetic stones their little sisters slide and click

from palm to palm. The two boys know they have to go.
They take the brightest lights, the ones for spotting

wildlife in the night and set out, slashing beams

across the world; decapitating trees and slicing boulders,
knocking stars down from the open terrifying sky,

until they reach the other door and slam it shut.

From the outgrown bunks of an outgrown room
we hear them laughing late into the night.

AMONG MY FATHER'S STORIES

Much is blamed on women.
How we wear our beauty, for example:
boldly; irresponsibly; flash and flaunt
or not at all: mouse dropping drab.
It's 1948; girls are singing,
wearing white,

a chorus from the upper school
of Saint-Some-Woman's-Name.
Christmastime in 1948.
They're singing in the overheated day room
of the V.A. Hospital in Richmond,
wearing white,

before an audience of men
all freshly bathed and listening.
Panes are fogged. Heat swirls and eddies:
disinfectant, taffeta, L'air du Temps, cold sweat.
It's close, the war is over, radiators hiss and girls
are singing in the overheated dayroom
wearing white,

the wounds aren't new; it's Christmastime.
A girl—so beautiful, this girl—
and here, my father's voice begins to crack—
so beautiful, this girl in white
at the end of a row of girls
wearing white,

leans toward the man who sits before her,
panes are fogged, and asks what song he'd like to hear.
He doesn't answer right away.

She waits and smiles.
1948, L'air du Temps, radiator hiss.
He answers, roughly, "Silent Night."

The girls begin to sing
and as they do, the man
who had not spoken in four years
begins to weep, the other men begin
to weep, my father
at the age of eighty-eight
begins to weep—

It's Christmastime in 1948,
and girls are singing,
wearing white.

FACT OR FICTION

His walking stick hooked
high in a branch
above the station platform:
fact.

No witnesses: *fact.*

The odd miracle
claps both hands on an old man's back.
Shock and feathers: a splintering,
his pain shattered, gone:
fiction.

Pigeons stutter into flight, circle,
no place to light: *fact.*

He is healed, whole.
He tosses the cane up.
He boards the train.
Fiction, fiction, fiction.

Astonished, his body rises
to the trees, boots brush through canopy
as he breaks into air,

his awestruck hands open,
letting fall the cane
back to earth

where it catches
on a branch,
a vaudevillian hook:
fiction, fact, dramatic simile.

A few leaves shake free,
kettle down.
Fact.

No warning bell. No whistle. *Fiction.*
Important to be ready for the road. *Fact.*

III

NIGHT: AWAITING NEWS

Cedars gather by the creek
in the old way—

shawled women,
self-contained, apart,
skirts brushing skirts.

Close by, a clutch
of leaves at woods' edge
silvers, twists
like a handkerchief
in anxious hands.

In the orchard: air stirs.

A voice, steady
on the telephone.

Each death will
redefine you.

SICKROOM

The pills look panicked,
wild-eyed,

packed together
in a vial like that

and every now and then
there's a shift,

a jostle for position
like ice in a glass,

a click, a note,
a tiny exhalation,

a sound you'd never notice
under other circumstances

but everything here
is magnified

like a spoon
tilted in a water glass,

and all of us designed
to dissolve.

NOTHING'S CHANGED

Yellow-cheeked cherries
in a cardboard boat, barely
a handful missing.

The ones I brought you
in a small blue dish.
Two days ago. Or was it three?

Everything else is still here—
your book and pencil,
eyeglasses, pillow, chair,
even the motes in the air.

Still here. Still here.
Everything else.
My hands that pitted the fruit.
My hands that smoothed back your hair.

HOSPICE SYMPTOM RELIEF KIT

Tucked behind the butter window
of your bone-white ice box—

a rainbow of glass vials
in a cardboard carton
with a red wax seal and a key
to their color-coded caps.

For weeks, not part
of the visible spectrum.

Ruby-throated hummingbird
at the sugar water, glimpsed, gone,
quick flash in the eye's corner
when rummaging lunch;

it was like that—
brown box in the window,
ruby seal, the end,
don't think until

it's time. The vials
were slender as a trumpet vine's
long throated blossoms,
blue for hallucination,
violet for pain,

swift nectar tipped
under your tongue.

The end suddenly colorful.
And you a bird.

NOT AN ABACUS

This is
not an
abacus,
a tally,
a rosary,
or prayer.
This is
how I
keep you
here, by
sliding
each short
hour, like
a bead
along
a string,
telling
and re-
telling,
service
by small
service,
the hours
of your
last days.
How I
read aloud
from *The
Interpreter
of Maladies*,
brought you
water, bits

of sweet fruit.
This is
not an
abacus,
a tally,
a rosary,
a prayer.

SELF-TIMER

I twist camera to tripod,
drag apparatus down the stairs
into my dining room,
wipe clean the lens.

I put a green chair in the corner,
set the switch.

I tell myself it's afternoon light I'm after,
another year down on its knees

                  a gauzy mood shot through the window,

          winter garden in late light,

                that sort of thing,

but the image centered
in the crosshairs of the focus box

is me: seated,
stripped to the waist

watching a red dot
flash, gain speed,
watching for the shutter's
eye-blink
while I can.

THE SHIP OF GRIEF RETURNS TO SHORE

and I am on it,
standing at the rail.
No end
to this cruise.

Alone, we disembark
at will, row
separate skiffs
to shore,
or not.

I mourn
the great ship's
metal bone of railing
in my hands,
the heavy doors,
the salt, the silence
of the crew but

I am ready
for this little boat.

WORK IN PROGRESS

Last night, without warning,
I dreamed the end of the world.
Its shattering white flashes
beyond the curve of earth
burned egg-yolk orange.

I ran to find my children but instead
I found my mother—two months
dead. Not possible.
But it was she: no oxygen,
no gasping, arms held out to me.

She wore my favorite nightgown.
I pressed my face into her neck,
breathed in her scent, her skin.
All day, I've wept; been happy.
I had not dreamed her until then.

RAIN-FILLED RUT

All sky. Earth flat
as a sympathy card.

At the turn between fields
where the track deepens,

my daughter crouches
above a pool

speckled with tadpoles.
She is immense

and small, peering down
at black bodies

powered by black lines
that do not yet

make her think of sperm
or consider herself

a bearer of eggs,
but only how her face

is a new moon in a tadpole sky.
One quick bird crosses

the bright behind her.
No clouds.

All the action's on the earth.
For a while.

PSEUDOCRIS CRUCIFER

I'm waiting for spring peepers,
backs emblazoned
with a tiny x, to rise
from cold beds of bark and leaf,
sniff out the ditches and begin
to jingle last year's unspent coins
inside their pockets, trilling
to the darkening earth where
all day, I've been working,
clearing springs for pale green cress
to grow, some unseen mark
upon my back or lung,
skunk cabbages around me
auguring their spears of stink
through pristine earth,
the scent of rot already on me,
in me, bitter first, before
the sweet—it's spring.

SMALL MEMORY

My mother is riding a bicycle
for the last time,

turning slow careful circles
around a sandy road

that ends abruptly at the sea.
She's seventy-three.

She lets go the handlebars,
claps twice like a magician,

and waves goodbye to me.

ONE THING I KNOW FOR SURE

Each year, the best blackberries
are found here, behind

the Ascended Up On High
On Route 13 Reformed
Free Independent Baptist Church,

hanging fat among their brambles,
shimmering, black as swooning shapes
on the border of vision

when the mind swims
and the body goes faint.

Heavy heads nod and sway.
I reach in, gather, drop
bundled sweetness, one by one,

into my pail, each berry rich with
liquid stomp and stain, with human
sound and sin and struggle-to-be-good,

the word made flesh, speaking
purple-tongued to my empty tin.

IV

21st CENTURY OPTIONS

On television: bombing's
busy aftermath with narration
in the clipped tones
of a BBC reporter-on-the-scene.
Between the one-two beat
of sirens and his perfect pitch,
I hear Bach's *Toccata and Fugue in D Minor*
and Mozart's *Rondo alla Turca*
accompanied by several unknown
melodies all ringing out
from cell phones inside
the pockets of the dead.

OUTBUILDING

Ridiculous to paint the door blue, plant
hollyhocks against this white-washed shambles
as though it were some cottage in the Cotswolds.
Inside, always the same weather: deep cold.
The more we scoured, the clearer it became.
Our hands and faces shining back at us,
reflected in the fat sides of rendering vats,
in the drains gleaming like stars in the floor.

But there was no polishing up
the meat hooks, row after row
of small black scythes
studding the beams above us.
No way to translate *abattoir* to anything
but what it is: our slaughterhouse.

NIGHT CRAWLERS

Morning: children shriek
the way to school.
Worms on the sidewalks,
pale pink bodies stretched blindly
across concrete, blacktop, hot sun
blinking between trees.
Three minutes of direct exposure
means they're toast.

Leaping wild, children dance
the dance of worm avoidance,
grind worms underfoot,
or peel up their sticky bodies,
place them gently in grass.

There's always a child who kills and only kills.
There's always a child who saves and only saves.
There's always a child, hunkered down
in the playground's corner
who establishes a hospital for worms,
who gathers worms brought by the merciful,
who places them tenderly in rows
and cuts them carefully
to pieces with a sharp wood chip.

I'M SORRY TO TELL YOU

but one year calamity
will bend back the bars
on your windows, step
inside, select a knife
from the jumble
in your kitchen drawer
or pull one from the pristine
block beside the stove
and hold it to your throat
until you walk
into the little waiting room
inside the self (no
clocks, no magazines)
where you will wait
to see what's left
when what is happening
is done. So curious,
the calm. Curious too,
that when calamity walks out,
it walks out through the door
like anybody else.
And the door, like any door,
ridiculous with locks,
clicks shut.

ALL RIGHT, FATE, THEN

I trapped a yellow jacket
in a jar held tight
against a window pane,
its spiky legs and stinger
snagging on the packet
of lettuce seeds
I slid across the open mouth
of the jar, and I,
magnanimous,
un-stung, walked out
into the world to set it free.
I whisked away
the paper door and it flew out
and straight down
into the dog's mouth,
snap, snap, pink tongue
licking black gums
and I'd thought
that old boy was asleep.

WATCH IN THE GARDEN

The night before the war began, my husband
found a wristwatch in the garden.

Dull gold among dull mulch, it shone a little.
Roman numerals, a classic face, the crystal

uncracked, and its alligator band still soft
enough to circle my wrist. I tried the catch,

it caught and held and even when I shook it
hard, it would not fall. I wiped it clean.

We let it lie between us on a linen towel,
we drank and talked. The mildness of the night

was strange but everything seemed strange.
War was coming. Lines drawn. Dates set.

So many things did not belong to us
yet they were here, and ours.

AT THE OPHTHALMOLOGIST

Eyes numbed with yellow drops
I consider the eye chart's architecture,
sort letters into categories—
columns, portals—noting slim distinctions,
how I might bend to step inside the O
or rest a shoulder on the doorjamb
of the D and sneak a smoke
but then I'm asked to name them
so I sit my mental self back down,
call each by name. I begin to see
how they've been held apart
in the solitary confinement of white space,
and how their ranks fall off into a vanishing point
that's upside down, can't force perspective,
won't add up, and suddenly the goddamn waste
outrages me—I know, I know,
let's buck up dear, it's not a bomb
exploding in a marketplace,
the corpses bulldozed daily into pits,
or pounds of pasta salad thrown out after parties—
no, it's you, just you, your thinning lenses,
egg-shaped eyes, inside a small room
with no windows, in a renovated town,
repeating: *dimmer, smaller, better, worse.*

SOMETHING FOR EVERYONE IN THE EGYPTIAN WING

I stand at the tomb's false door,
its threshold like an empty stoop,
and read that what is left here,
will be taken up and used by the dead
at their considerable leisure.
The dead require life force.
Otherwise, they wander, seeking
honey cakes and veal shanks, eau de vie,
pot stickers, corn dogs, yams,
hard-boiled eggs like eyeballs soaked in beet juice,
tamarinds and good Bordeaux,
stumbling through back yards
with their zombie knack
for catastrophic timing in the lives of
realtors inside empty houses
or horny high school seniors in their cars.
Who knew those arms outstretched with awful nails
were reaching for the pantry, not for us?
Still, it seems wise to keep them put,
lay out the bread and wine and alabaster jars
of fragrant oil, each in its particular place
carved into stone. Consider
the one-way beauty of a painted eye,
a hinge-less door, a threshold into stone.
We make our offerings then beat
a swift retreat back into sex
and real estate, hands emptied
of their casseroles and layered dips,
our fingernails alternately manicured
tipped or chewed down to the quick.

MIDWAY

The two-headed pig was jammed into a jar
so I couldn't tell it from the cat

with two bodies or the cloven-hoofed
devil baby discovered dead in a dumpster

in New Jersey. But Angel, the Snake Girl
was alive. No arms, no legs, no bones in her body.

The word *illusion* floated pale grey,
like a misty ocean underneath her name,

but I was distracted by two men hosing down
the world's smallest horse and I only

remembered that later. Snake Girl *was* alive,
a woman in her twenties, her head stuck

through a hole in a fake table and wound
around with perfect fake snake coils.

She wore her hair in bangs and flicked her eyes
from side to side but mostly she looked tired.

I asked her how she was. She answered: *cold.*
After that, there wasn't much to say. I stayed.

The horse looked like a stumpy long-necked dog
and it was clear to me now: I was part of the show.

PATHWAY

One evening, before rain, we pulled up grass
between slate stepping stones and planted
creeping thyme, dwarf mint and chamomile
instead. The path led to a gate, the gate
to our garden: shady, ivied, fenced.
We'd read of such a fragrant pathway
in a book. At dusk, the lovers, though not yet,
had walked it, wordlessly, bare-footed, back
toward the lights and voices of a house,
each press of their steps releasing scent.
You bought the herbs at a roadside stand;
we planted them together. A shame, the way
we never tended it; how grass returned,
became this path of blades we tend with blades.

STORM, AND AFTER

Overheated room and talk and talk
and no one listening.
Steady drumbeat in the downspouts,
tuneful as monsoon rain in a Graham Greene book.
I wash my sticky hands
in a white sink above a beheaded broccoli.
Everyone's trying so hard.

Later, warm wind
lifts leaves of the pin oaks
as I walk to my car.
Lines of ragged clouds lit by town lights
chase after the storm,

and through them I see giant stars
so freshly washed, it's clear
there's nothing between us but distance.

GROUNDHOG WARS, YEAR THREE

Hand to hand combat now.
You're back, a low-to-the-ground
lesson to be learned year after year,
your arrival timed precisely with the
succulent blooming of Canterbury bells.
You, who are undeterred by boards and wire,
who digs a house beneath my house,
who eats the buds before they bloom,
who I didn't catch when you were young
and dumb enough to eat the apples
smeared with honey in my HavAHart,
who I can't shoot because I live in town
next door to a retired cop who knows
the sound of small arms fire. He offered,
this year, if I poisoned you, to pull you
out from underneath the porch
when you began to stink (he's dragged
worse bodies from worse spots,
he says) so I mix arsenic and chunky
peanut butter, make country paté, push
a dish of it beneath the porch and find
today you've sucked the peanut butter
off each pellet, spat them back into the dish
and pushed it out into the rosemary
for me or mine to eat and die.

WHAT IT COMES DOWN TO

The clock on the stove sounds out
machine gun fire—
a ratchet up from yesterday's
stick against a picket fence
and now the damn thing's counting out
the heartbeats of entire days in minutes.

I used to give the stovetop one good whack
and chastened silence would return,
but not today: the mechanism's mad,
it's always telling time, it might as well just
pound its hands against the glass
and I can't make it stop
unless I shut the whole works down

but then I'd have to face the pale skin
of this half-cooked bird,
the bowl of naked peas, the cut-down herbs,
the new potatoes softly scrubbed and patted dry
lined up along the oven's rim

as well as those of you who came to eat.
So once again it all comes down
to turning up the music.

RX

You'll never get your ass back in those pants,
try though you will, that time is gone, it's true.
Do you want Zoloft or an Ativan?

No one need know if you're depressed or an-
xious; if this is pathological or mood.
To never get your ass back in those pants

is catastrophic, yes, and evidence
of age—my God, so's death—and coming soon.
OK. Try Zoloft first, (save Ativan)

so quiet, sweet and swift, its dance
on tightrope synapses in tiny shoes.
You'll never get your ass back in those pants

but you won't *care* and that's a stronger stance
than *caring* is—and with a war on, too!
Zoloft (or Prozac), with an Ativan's

the perfect antidote to turbulence
from age, war, gluttony and fear. Taboo
your guilt and love your ass; donate the pants!
Start Zoloft; you can always up the Ativan.

ANOTHER EASTER

The bones of the buck lie where he lay
by the creek last fall, wounded, licking water.
Small mound of carcass in the meadow's sweep
sunken, smaller now, undistinguishable

from the wrack of winter wheat.
No flag left, spine bare, stiff fringe across the ribs,
his strong legs stripped and milk-pod pale.
Seeds of his last meal deep in rot.

And so it is with our grief.
Extended exhalations, slow dissolves,
the stubborn skull protecting memory,
like last meat, in a bony cave.

And something rooting down
inside, ready to rise.

LAST WILL

When I am ash, as is my wish,
take a stone out to the field for me
and leave it near the meadow wall
where it won't jam machinery.

Nothing cut or polished. Something
tumbled down the stream and smoothed
with sand will do, the sort of stone
that's been there all along. It's just

that in the field tonight, I stopped
and stood beyond the cedars
in the hedgerow's coils and twists—
the heart-shaped lump of a wasp nest

suspended from a maple branch above
my own dark shape—and the moon's
unclouded eye fell on us all so equally,
it seemed as good a place as any I could be.

ACKNOWLEDGMENTS

Grateful acknowledgement is made to the editors of the following publications where these poems, some in slightly altered form, first appeared:

5 A.M.: "Day Players in the Makeup Trailer," "RX 2005"
Rattle: "Self-Portrait With the Smithfield Ham We Had to Cut on the Bandsaw"
Drunken Boat: "Fact or Fiction," "Your Suicide Script"
Margie: "Hospice Symptom Relief Kit," "21st Century Options," "Waking,"
Nimrod: "Tips For Domestic Travel"
Philadelphia Stories: "Renovation," "Colloquy in the Heat," Midway"
Mad Poets Review: "The Ship of Grief Returns to Shore," "I'm Sorry to Tell You."

"Clothesline" first appeared in the anthology *Hands Offering Bread* (Bucks County Poet Laureate Program). "The Book of Years," "Self-Portrait With the Smithfield Ham..." and "Tips for Domestic Travel" won the Robert Fraser Poetry Award in 2005.

My gratitude to Stirling Spadea and Eden Spadea for permission to use the painting "Untitled" and to Ann Combs for her assistance.

My thanks to all those who read this manuscript or offered advice on particular poems, especially Christopher Bursk, Lynn Levin, Robert Bense, Eric Pankey and Amy Gerstler. Thanks to Liam Rector, Ed Ochester and Henri Cole for guidance and to Diane Goettel and Black Lawrence Press for belief in this book. My gratitude to the Bucks County poetry community for constant support and special thanks to Niloufar Talebi, Trudy Ames and Leslie McGrath for their generous friendship. Thank you, Reb, for everything.

Hayden Saunier grew up in Charlottesville, Virginia and is a graduate of the University of Virginia and the Bennington Writing Seminars MFA program. An actress and a teacher, she is a Pushcart Prize nominee and winner of the 2005 Robert Fraser Poetry Competition. She lives in Bucks County, Pennsylvania, with her husband and two children. *Tips For Domestic Travel* was a finalist for several awards, including the St Lawrence Book Award.